Planning for Your Special Needs Child

Planning for Your Special Needs Child

Amy Newman, Esq.

Real Life Legal™

Helpful Guides for Everyday Legal Matters

Parker Press Inc.

Contents

Contents

What This Book's About

If you are the parent of a special needs child, you already know that you face different challenges than other parents. For starters, you must face health and planning issues early on. Here we will share the wisdom of those who have walked this path before you.

When you have a child, your thoughts turn to the future—will he be athletic like mom or musical like dad? Will she be a star pupil with her pick of universities, or will she choose to attend a trade or vocational school? Will she meet a nice man and have a family, or focus just on her career and break every glass ceiling? The possibilities are endless, and one of parenting's greatest joys is watching your child's future unfold before your eyes.

But if your child has special needs—whether autism, cerebral palsy, Down's syndrome or some other disability—then your thoughts about your child's future are markedly different.

- Will he be self-sufficient?

- How will we afford his medical care and equipment?

- Who will help when we can no longer lift her?

- Who will take care of her when we die?

Watching your child grow can still bring great joy, but it can be tinged with a mixture of fear, anxiety and even a bit of sadness.

Raising children is scary. Raising a special needs child can be even scarier. And if you are reading this book, you've no doubt asked yourself many, if not more, of these questions. You want to be proactive about your child's future, but you may not know where to start—or even that you need to start. That's where this book can help.

Whether your child is two, twenty-two or forty-two, it is never too early or too late to start planning for a special needs child.

Here we take a look at the ins and outs of planning for your child's future, from the importance of creating trusts to maintain eligibility for **"Medicaid"** and other needs-based public assistance, to obtaining guardianship of your child when he turns eighteen years of age, and doing estate planning for when you can no longer care for your child.

Government Benefits

The availability of certain benefits and planning tips may depend on your child's age. In this book, we'll let you know if the programs and benefits we talk about are limited to a certain age or condition.

What Does "Special Needs" Mean?

We use the term "special needs" to mean a child who needs extra support or intervention. This is typically caused by a health condition that impacts your child's ability to function the way "normal" children do.

The term **"special needs"** usually refers to any person who is not "neurotypical"–that is, typically developing, in either gross motor, fine motor or cognitive abilities. Special needs children generally require early intervention, special education and other specialized services and supports.

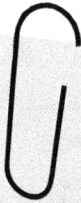

Special Needs Conditions

A child can have "special needs" for a variety of reasons including:

- Genetic conditions, such as Down's syndrome or Sotos syndrome.

- Conditions a child is born with such as cerebral palsy or spina bifida.

- Mental health conditions.

- Intellectual disabilities.

- "Invisible" disabilities (e.g., autism) that may not be immediately apparent but affect the individual's ability to function in everyday life.

- Complex medical conditions such as cancer.

Special needs can also refer to people who require specialized services, support or monitoring due to a complex medical condition. For example, a child with a heart condition or cancer may have no physical or cognitive disabilities, but will have special needs.

For purposes of this book, when we refer to "special needs," we mean those children who may:

- Require specialized services and supports, and require assistance with **"Activities of Daily Living."**

- Have complex medical conditions that subject them to frequent medical monitoring.

- Meet the disability definition/criteria for needs-based public assistance, such as Medicaid, **"Supplemental Security Income (SSI)"** or **"Social Security Disability Income (SSDI),"** whether or not they actually qualify due to financial eligibility guidelines.

Not "One Size Fits All"

There is no "one size fits all" when determining whether a child with a particular disability will qualify for public benefits. A common question is: "My child was diagnosed with X disability—will she qualify for SSI and Medicaid?" It is not enough to simply be disabled in order to receive benefits; rather, the disability must negatively impact your child's daily life.

As disabled children become adults, the criteria for receiving public assistance changes. For a child, the question asked is whether the disability "negatively impacts," your child's daily life. As a child grows into adulthood, the question often asked is whether the disability interferes with a person's ability to engage in gainful employment. One child with a specific diagnosis

Activities of Daily Living (ADL)

ADLs are basic tasks of everyday life, such as eating, bathing, dressing, toileting and transferring from sitting to standing. A person's ability when it comes to ADLs is an important factor in determining availability of public assistance benefits.

may require lifelong care, while another may be able to fully participate in everyday life with few modifications and little assistance.

SSI and Medicaid eligibility determinations are based on how a particular disability impacts your child, not just that your child has a disability.

The **"Social Security Administration (SSA)"** has created a list of **"Compassionate Allowances,"** which are medical conditions and diagnoses that automatically meet the SSI definition of disability. The list currently contains approximately 200 such allowances. http://www.ssa.gov/compassionateallowances

Special Needs Planning: Do I Need a Lawyer?

Not all aspects of special needs planning require a lawyer, but some do. A lawyer is likely needed for estate planning and creating supplemental trusts for your child, but you may be able to apply for public assistance on your own.

When planning for a special needs child, there are some aspects of planning that require a lawyer. Others you can manage on your own. In an era of "do it yourself," downloadable, legal documents, it may be tempting to do estate planning on your own. But don't! Too much is at stake with a special needs child, and it's important to have estate plans done properly.

You Need a Lawyer for Estate Planning with a Special Needs Child

It is essential to engage a lawyer with experience in trusts, estates and special needs planning to get the job done right for your child and your family. Even a small mistake can have enormous consequences that could adversely affect your child's future eligibility for Medicaid, choice of guardian when you die and management of his or her financial resources.

Many people think that estate planning isn't such a big deal.

My spouse and I are leaving everything we have to each other, and then to our kids. My sister or his brother will take care of the kids, if they're still young. Why should I bother with estate planning? I can use the money for something else.

For a typical parent that may work out fine, but for the parent of a special needs child, this type of thinking is a huge mistake.

If you have a special needs child, you need to be proactive where your child is concerned. Every aspect of life requires planning, and it is up to you to be in the driver's seat.

Estate planning, which is discussed in greater detail at the end of this book, must be undertaken early on when you have a special needs child. You cannot assume that your loved ones will have the resources or wherewithal to take over for you. Failure to plan for your child's future can have unanticipated and unintended consequences that will be difficult, if not impossible, to fix. For example:

- Did you know that if you leave funds outright to a special needs child who is receiving Medicaid or Supplemental Security Income (SSI), those benefits will disappear until he or she has spent almost every penny of the inheritance?

- If you never applied for Medicaid benefits on behalf of a special needs child, because you took care of the child and paid the bills, what will happen when you are not there?

  - Who will be your child's guardian? If you don't have a will or appointment in place, a court will decide who among your family and friends that step up to take your place is the most appropriate—and it may not be the person you would have chosen.

  - There will be no supports in place, such as respite, adult day rehabilitation, or personal care attendants, who can help a newly appointed guardian care for him or her.

You know how much you do for your child on a daily basis. You owe it to your child to have a plan in place when you're no longer around. And you need an attorney well skilled in all aspects of special needs benefits and estate planning to work with you to formulate a plan.

REAL LIFE EXAMPLE

Mary is seventy years old. Her son, Ethan, is forty-two and has Down's syndrome; he is unemployed and receives SSI and Medicaid. Mary has cared for Ethan her entire life and was appointed his guardian when he turned eighteen. Mary has an estate worth about $235,000 and Ethan is her only child. Mary never wrote a Will and when she died suddenly of a heart attack, Ethan inherited her entire estate outright.

Because this inheritance constitutes an additional resource, Ethan loses both his SSI and Medicaid. He cannot reapply for these benefits until he has spent the inheritance down below the state's $2,000 resource limit. When he finally regains eligibility, he has no assets to use as a safety net to pay for medical services Medicaid does not cover, and no money to pay for things like museum trips, baseball games, and the annual Disneyland vacation they both enjoyed. This is not the life Mary would have wanted for Ethan, and it could have been avoided if Mary had drawn a proper estate plan for her future and Ethan's future.

A lawyer knowledgeable in special needs and trust law can structure your estate plan to enable your child to simultaneously benefit from the inheritance and maintain eligibility for public benefits.

It's better to spend the time and money on a lawyer now and make sure your estate plan is properly drafted, rather than have your child (or his or her guardian) spend even more time and money after you're gone trying to fix it.

You Can Apply for Benefits and Public Assistance Without a Lawyer

If you engage an attorney with expertise in special needs estate planning, he or she will often assist with applications for your child to receive needs-based public assistance. However, the actual application for public benefits is something you can do on your own. Medicaid applications can be found on your state's Department of Health and Human Services website, or by going into the local Medicaid office and requesting a copy.

Applications for Supplemental Security Income (SSI) or Social Security Disability Income (SSDI) can also be found online at the Social Security Administration (SSA) website, http://www.ssa.gov/disabilityssi, or at your local SSA office. Local agencies that serve the special needs community can often help you complete the application or can point you in the direction of a care coordinator who can. Your local Medicaid or SSA office may even have a list of providers. Even better, these services are usually provided free of charge.

Getting Needs-Based Public Assistance for Your Child

With a special needs child, you'll want to explore benefits under federal, state and local public assistance programs. Often they impose limits on benefits if you have other resources.

For your child to qualify for most forms of needs-based public assistance, you must meet income, resource and disability eligibility requirements. The most common public assistance programs are Medicaid (which goes by different names in different states), Supplemental Security Income (SSI) and Social Security Disability Income (SSDI). There may be others in your state or community.

All of these programs limit the amount of income and assets (resources) that you can have and still receive benefits.

Supplemental Security Income and Social Security Disability Income

"Supplemental Security Income (SSI)" is a federal income supplement program that makes monthly payments to individuals who are low income or have limited resources.

Although SSI is a federally mandated program, it is administered at the state level and the amount of SSI payments varies depending on where you live, with some states providing more generous benefits than others. It is funded through general tax revenues, not social security taxes, and is therefore not the same as social security retirement benefits.

Those who are disabled will qualify for SSI if the income/resource limits are met. Those age sixty-five and older or who are blind are also eligible for SSI benefits.

"Social Security Disability Income (SSDI)" is a federally funded government program that employees pay into via mandatory payroll deductions. SSDI pays benefits to disabled workers and certain members of their family who are insured due to their work history. There are no income and resource requirements. Instead, payment of benefits is based solely on disability, which is determined according to the SSDI rules.

A parent's SSDI benefits can be paid to a disabled child of any age, if the child was diagnosed with the disability before turning twenty-two years of age, and if the parent either: (i) dies, (ii) becomes disabled before age sixty-five and receives benefits or (iii) receives SSI retirement benefits.

Total Disability Required

SSI and SSDI only provide benefits for total disability, not partial disability.

- If your child is injured at work, and is expected to be able to resume work in six months, he will be ineligible to receive benefits.

- SSI and SSDI only pay for a disability that is expected to last for more than 12 months.

Income and Resource Limits for SSI Eligibility

When determining financial eligibility for SSI, your child's age determines whether or not your income and resources will be counted. If your child is under the age of eighteen, the value of your income and resources will be added to your child's; if the combined total exceeds the allowable limits, your child will be denied benefits.

If your child is eighteen years of age or older—even if he or she lives with you—your income and resources will not be counted as his or hers. Your child's financial eligibility will be determined solely by his or her own income and resources.

To give you an idea of allowable resources, for 2014, a child under the age of eighteen was allowed to have $1,750 in monthly income and still meet SSI's income eligibility guideline. An adult age eighteen or older could not earn more than $1,070 per month. The allowable monthly income changes annually. The current total allowable resources are $2,000 for an individual and $3,000 for a married couple. If a child under age eighteen lives at home with parents, the first $2,000 (or $3,000, if living with both parents) of parents' resources are not counted against the limits.

What counts as income and what counts as a resource when determining eligibility? Types of countable income include:

- Wages or self-employment earnings.

- Pension payments.

- Interest income.

- Cash gifts.

- State disability payments.

- Food, shelter or other items received for free or for less than fair market value.

- Portion of income from spouse or parents that is counted toward total income.

Assets that *may* count as resources for SSI eligibility include:

- Cash.

- Bank accounts, stocks and U.S. savings bonds.

- Land.

- Life insurance.

- Personal property.

- Vehicles or boats.

Assets also include other property that could be converted to cash and used for food or shelter. One can also have assets that are deemed resources because they come from a spouse, parent or parent's spouse (even if not the child's parent.)

Assets that *may not* be counted as resources for SSI eligibility include:

- A home and its accompanying land.

- Household furnishings and personal items (such as a couch or wedding ring).

- Burial plots or burial funds (up to $1,500).

- Life insurance policies with a combined face value of $1,500 or less.

- One vehicle if used to transport the applicant and a household member.

- Grants, scholarships, fellowships or other gifts to pay educational expenses incurred in the nine months following receipt.

Resources are calculated at the start of each month, and if your child is over-resourced at the start of the month, he will be ineligible to receive benefits for the duration of the month. Any income he receives must be spent during the month it is received or put into a self-settled trust, discussed ahead.

SSI & SSDI Disability Determination

Whether your child is considered disabled for purposes of receiving SSI or SSDI benefits depends on his or her age.

Children under the age of eighteen are considered disabled if they have:

A medically determinable, physical or mental impairment that results in marked and severe functional limitations, and which can be expected to result in death or which has lasted or can be expected to last for a continuous period of not less than twelve months.

Physical or mental impairment includes any "impairment that results from anatomical, physiological or psychological abnormalities" that can be proven by any medically accepted clinical or laboratory diagnostic technique.

Children eighteen years of age or older will be considered disabled for purposes of SSI and SSDI if they are:

Unable to engage in any substantial gainful activity due to any medically determinable physical or mental impairment which can be expected to result in death or which has lasted or can be expected to last for a continuous period of not less than twelve months.

Gainful Activity is Not Only Work

Your child does not need to be working a full-time job to be considered gainfully employed. SSA considers gainful work activity to be any work:

- Performed for pay or profit;
- Generally performed for pay or profit; or
- Intended for profit, whether or not a profit is realized.

In determining whether your child engages in substantial gainful activity, SSA will deduct from your child's monthly earnings an amount equal to the money your child must pay for car services, medical devices, equipment, prostheses and similar items and services in order to help him or her work. SSA generally considers earnings that exceed the allowable monthly income (which changes annually) to be the result of substantial gainful activity.

An Adult Disabled Child's Benefits Through a Parent's Status

An adult disabled child may be eligible to receive SSI payments if his parent is either deceased or receives retirement or SSDI benefits. Although the benefit is paid based on the parent's social security earnings record, the SSA refers to it as the child's benefit. In order to be eligible, the adult child must be unmarried, age eighteen or older and the disability must have occurred prior to the child's twenty-second birthday.

REAL LIFE EXAMPLE

Gabriel is thirty-three and lives with his parents. He was in a car accident at age twenty-three that left him severely disabled and unable to work. Gabriel's parents began receiving Social Security retirement benefits at age sixty-two. Because Gabriel's disability did not begin prior to his twenty-second birthday, he is not entitled to receive a disabled child's SSI payment.

Evelyn is twenty-seven years old and was born with spina bifida. She is unmarried and has never worked. Evelyn's mother began collecting Social Security retirement benefits at age sixty-two. Because Evelyn's disability began prior to her twenty-second birthday (she was born with it), Evelyn is entitled to receive a disabled child's SSI payment based on her mother's social security earnings.

Applying for SSI and SSDI Benefits

Your child's application for SSI or SSDI is submitted to your local SSA field office. The application includes:

- Identifying information about your child.

- Description of your child's disability.

- Financial information.

- Contact information for relevant medical providers.

- Other relevant information regarding his disability.

The SSA field office confirms non-medical information in the application and then forwards it to **"Disability Determination Services (DDSs)."** The DDSs are state agencies, funded by the federal government, responsible for collecting medical evidence and making the initial disability determination. The DDSs obtain medical information from your child's medical providers; if it is insufficient to make a disability determination, they can request that your child submit to a consultative examination.

Once all the information has been obtained, a two-person team, comprised of a medical or psychological consultant and a disability examiner, determines whether the applicant is disabled pursuant to SSI. If your child is determined disabled, the field office will calculate the amount of payment and begin sending benefits. If your child is denied benefits, you have the right to appeal the decision.

Medicaid Benefits for a Special Needs Child

Medicaid is a joint federal-state program that provides medical benefits to low-income, disabled and certain other populations. Within federal guidelines, states determine who is covered and the services they may receive.

Although mandated by the federal government, each state determines which services it will cover, eligibility standards and categories of individuals who will be covered, in alignment with broad federal guidelines. States are required to provide coverage to certain population groups, and are given the option to cover other groups.

Medicaid and Your State

Although Medicaid is a federally authorized program, states may choose to broaden the reach of their individual programs to cover more people or provide more services.

- They can also apply to Centers for Medicare & Medicaid Services (CMS) for a waiver that allows them to expand health coverage beyond these groups.

- Be sure to contact your local Medicaid office to determine your state's specific eligibility guidelines and what services are covered.

Children can qualify for Medicaid even if they have insurance coverage through their parents, their employers or their spouses. In these instances, Medicaid would be the child's secondary insurance, and would pay for covered services only after the primary insurance has paid its share of all claims. If your child does not have any other form of health insurance, Medicaid will be the primary health insurance. Not all medical providers accept Medicaid, so it is important to check prior to the visit that Medicaid is accepted.

State Medicaid programs must provide certain benefits, although there may be variations among states as to the amount, duration and scope of services that are covered. Federal law requires that state Medicaid programs cover the following services:

- Inpatient hospital services.

- Outpatient hospital services.

- Early and Periodic Screening, Diagnostic, and Treatment Services (EPSTD) for children under age twenty-one (includes dental, vision and hearing screens).

- Nursing facility services (skilled nursing, rehabilitation or long-term care).

- Home health services.

- Physician services.

- Rural health clinic services.

- Federally qualified health center services.

- Laboratory and X-ray services.

- Family planning services.

- Nurse midwife services.

- Certified pediatric and family nurse practitioner services.

- Freestanding birth center services.

- Transportation to medical care (generally Medicaid will only pay for travel to the closest treatment center).

- Tobacco cessation counseling for pregnant women.

Each state may also expand its program's coverage and provide optional benefits. Be sure to review your state Medicaid handbook or contact your Medicaid caseworker to determine whether and to what extent your state covers any of these optional benefits:

- Prescription drugs (although an optional benefit, currently all states cover outpatient prescription drugs to most Medicaid recipients).

- Clinic services.

- Physical therapy.

- Occupational therapy.

- Speech, hearing and language disorder services.

- Respiratory care services.

- Other diagnostic, screening, preventive and rehabilitative services.

- Podiatry services.

- Optometry services.

- Dental services (required for children under age twenty-one, optional for adults).

- Dentures.

- Prosthetics.

- Eyeglasses.

- Chiropractic services.

- Other practitioner services.

- Private duty nursing services.

- Personal care.

- Hospice.

- Case management.

- Services for individuals age sixty-five or older who are institutionalized with a mental disease.

- Intermediate-care facility services for individuals with mental impairments.

- Home- and community-based waiver services.

- Self-directed personal assistance services.

- Community first choice option (provides home and community-based attendant services to individuals with disabilities).

- Tuberculosis-related services.

- Inpatient psychiatric services for individuals under age twenty-one.

Medicaid Eligibility Based on Low Income

Eligibility for Medicaid based solely on income is determined by the **"Federal Poverty Level (FPL)."** As of January 1, 2014, the Affordable Care Act expanded Medicaid's reach by creating a national minimum eligibility level of 133% of FPL. In 2014, the FPL was $31,720.50 for a family of four (everywhere except Alaska and Hawaii).

Medicaid vs. Medicare

Medicaid and Medicare are two separate government programs that provide health care benefits.

- Medicare generally provides health benefits to individuals age sixty-five or older.

- Medicaid serves low-income and/or disabled individuals.

People can receive both Medicare and Medicaid if they meet the eligibility criteria for both. Disabled children may also qualify for Medicare, if their disability occurred before age twenty-two and their parents receive Medicare.

When determining eligibility, the income and resources of every household member is taken into account. The income and resources allowed vary among states, but a general rule of thumb is to apply the SSI income and resource limits.

However, certain resources (amounts vary among states) are not countable resources and are exempt for the purpose of determining Medicaid eligibility. These include:

- Personal vehicle.

- Your home.

- Household belongings.

- Pre-paid funeral account.

- Cemetery plot.

Medicaid Eligibility Based on Disability

Like SSI, Medicaid covers individuals with disabilities. In thirty-two states plus the District of Columbia, individuals who are eligible for SSI are automatically eligible to receive Medicaid, and only a single application is required. Alaska, Idaho, Kansas, Nebraska, Nevada, Oregon, Utah and the Northern Mariana Islands automatically grant Medicaid benefits to SSI recipients; however, they require separate applications for both. In these cases, the disability determination is the same as SSI.

The eigibility criteria in Connecticut, Hawaii, Illinois, Indiana, Minnesota, Missouri, New Hampshire, North Dakota, Ohio, Oklahoma and Virginia is more restrictive than that used by the SSA. In these states, receipt of SSI is not an automatic guarantee of Medicaid coverage.

TEFRA Medicaid State Plan Option/ Katie Beckett Waiver

Created under the **"Tax Equity and Fiscal Responsibility Act (TEFRA),"** TEFRA Medicaid, as it is more commonly known, is a special Medicaid program for children with long-term disabilities who are ineligible for SSI or traditional Medicaid due to their parents' income. Before the Katie Beckett Waiver, parents would be forced to institutionalize their child to get them the care they needed, since children who are institutionalized are Medicaid eligible regardless of their parents' income and resources.

For many families, the cost of their child's medical care and equipment is prohibitive, despite being financially ineligible for SSI and Medicaid.

In 1981, in response to the case of Katie Beckett, President Ronald Regan signed the Katie Beckett Waiver provision under TEFRA. In 1982, Congress created a state plan option under TEFRA that gave states the option to cover children whose disabilities qualified them for institutionalized care, but whose parents chose to care for them at home. The law was created so that these children would be able to remain at home with their families, without giving up access to the care and support they would receive if they were in an institution. Today the names "Katie Beckett Waiver" and "TEFRA" are used interchangeably.

The Katie Beckett Story

When Katie Beckett was five months old, she contracted encephalitis, a viral brain infection. While in the hospital she had a seizure and went into severe respiratory distress. A second seizure five hours later put her in a coma and she was placed on life support. The encephalitis then attacked Katie's central nervous system, paralyzing her diaphragm and making it impossible for her to breathe or swallow without medical support.

During her three-year hospitalization, Katie became eligible for both SSI and Medicaid. When her parents met their $1 million lifetime insurance cap, Medicaid covered the cost of Katie's care in full. When she was finally discharged, her Medicaid coverage stopped. Since their insurance limit was reached, her parents' only two options were to pay the cost of her care out of pocket or place Katie in an institution so Medicaid would once again cover her cost of care. Instead, her parents chose to challenge the rules so that Katie could receive the care she needed in the comfort of her own home, surrounded by her family.

Unlike SSI and traditional Medicaid, TEFRA Medicaid does not count the parents' income and resources against the child. Eligibility is instead based solely on the child's income and resource levels and the disability. In order to be eligible for TEFRA disability, your child must meet all of the following conditions:

- Be eighteen years of age or younger and live at home.

- Meet the SSI income and resource limits.

- Require a **"Level of Care (LOC)"** normally provided in a hospital, skilled nursing facility or intermediate-care facility (including an intermediate-care facility for people with intellectual disabilities).

- Have a disability that is terminal or expected to last more than twelve months (the SSI definition of disability).

- Be able to safely live at home.

In addition, the cost of care in the community must not exceed the cost of institutional care. In this context, "care in the community" means care at home or on an outpatient basis, rather than in an institutional setting.

States are not required to adopt TEFRA disability waiver provisions, and not all have done so. A few have created their own "look-alike" program under state law, similar to the federal program but generally providing services to more children. As of the date of this printing, the following have adopted a TEFRA waiver disability program or enacted their own look-alike program:

Alaska	Michigan	Pennsylvania
Arkansas	Minnesota	Rhode Island
District of Columbia	Mississippi	South Carolina
	Nebraska	South Dakota
Georgia	Nevada	Vermont
Idaho	New Hampshire	West Virginia
Massachusetts	Oklahoma	Wisconsin

Phil and Susie have a six-year-old daughter, Elizabeth, who has cerebral palsy. They earn $125,000 per year, own a home worth $435,000, cars valued at $25,000, have $150,000 in savings and another $500,000 in various stocks, bonds and retirement plans. Their assets put them well above Medicaid's income and resource limits.

Phil and Susie have health insurance through their employer, but it doesn't cover most of Elizabeth's therapies and medical equipment, leaving Phil and Susie with tens of thousands of out-of-pocket medical costs per year.

However, Phil and Susie are lucky. They live in Massachusetts, which has adopted TEFRA waiver provisions. Their income and resources are completely disregarded for the purposes of qualifying Elizabeth for Medicaid. The only factors are Elizabeth's income (which is zero), resources (a $500 savings account) and disability. Therefore, Elizabeth would qualify under Massachusetts TEFRA program, and the majority of her medical expenses will be covered.

Home- and Community-Based Waivers

Medicaid waivers are optional programs that allow states to waive traditional eligibility rules in order to provide coverage to more people. Waivers cover services that otherwise would not be provided. States can pick and choose which waivers they wish to implement, and establish different eligibility groups within each waiver.

"Home- and Community-Based Waivers (HCBW)" allow states to provide individuals who have qualifying disabilities, with long-term care services at home or in the community, instead of in an institutional setting. Services that may be available under the HCBW include:

- Case management.

- Home health aide.

- Personal care attendant.

- Adult day health services.

- Day or residential habilitation.

- Respite care.

Each waiver under the HCBW umbrella provides services to individuals with similar needs, such as children with complex medical needs or individuals with intellectual and developmental disabilities, and each offers a different set of services. Enrollment in this program often permits recipients to apply for state mini-grant funding. These funds can be used to pay for things that neither Medicaid nor the HCBW cover, such as home modifications and non-covered therapies.

Receipt of waiver services is not automatic. Once your child is approved for Medicaid, you will need to apply for each specific waiver. As always, it is important to check with your state Medicaid office to determine which programs are available and the eligibility criteria for each.

Applying for Medicaid

Getting children qualified for Medicaid requires more than simply completing forms and sending them, along with a statement of diagnosis from their pediatricians, to a local Medicaid office. The process can be somewhat overwhelming the first time you apply.

When you first visit your local Medicaid office to pick up an application, be sure to ask for a list of service agencies or local care coordinators that can help walk you through the process. But until then, here is a rough guide as to what you can expect.

Medicaid Application Process

In addition to providing identifying information about your child, the application is where you list all of your child's income and resources and, if you are applying for Medicaid based on your family income, the income and resources of each person living in your household. You must also inform Medicaid of any private health insurance anybody in your household has, or has access to. You will also need to provide financial statements and documents identifying the value of your resources, as well as pay stubs or W-2 forms that verify income.

If your child is applying for TEFRA Medicaid, you will only need to complete the financial information as it pertains to your child. Since eligibility is based solely on your child's income and resources, you do not need to include the income or resources of anybody else living in your household.

State Disability Determination

The Medicaid disability determination is made each year, by your state. Similar to the SSI disability determination, each year you submit a disability determination form providing information about your child's disability and the contact information for all relevant medical providers to your local Medicaid office.

Level of Care Determination

If you are seeking TEFRA Medicaid benefits for your child, the state must make a level of care (LOC) determination. Because the purpose of the TEFRA Medicaid option is to allow children who would otherwise qualify for in-patient services to instead receive those services and supports at home or in the community, the LOC determination must find that your child requires care that rises to the care provided in an acute care hospital, nursing facility, intermediate care facility for individuals with intellectual and developmental disabilities or an inpatient psychiatric hospital.

Depending on the nature of your child's disability, the LOC may be completed as frequently as every year or as infrequently as every three to five years. The LOC determination generally includes an in-home interview that goes into detail about your child's daily level of care.

Planning for the Future: Using Trusts

If you establish a supplemental or special needs trust for your child, you can preserve public assistance benefits. Funds in the trust can be used to provide for things that public assistance doesn't cover.

In addition to pursuing public assistance for your special needs child, you'll want to consider creating a special needs trust to plan for your child's future. It can be an invaluable way to make legally enforceable plans for the future. With a properly drafted trust you can:

- Appoint a guardian to care for your child at your death.

- Appoint a trustee to manage your child's inheritance.

- Dictate how your estate should be distributed to your child, including how much he or she should get and when, and the types of allowable distributions.

- Ensure there are funds available for your child to go on vacation, attend school, attend sporting events, or participate in any other activity that would enrich his or her life.

For special needs children, a properly drafted special needs trust maintains their current and future eligibility for needs-based public assistance and ensures that there are funds available to pay for medical treatment Medicaid doesn't cover.

Using a Trust That Preserves Public Assistance

In many respects the trusts created to preserve eligibility for needs-based public assistance are the same as trusts created for non-special needs reasons. Each type of trust has the same parties: grantor, beneficiary and trustee. They also have specific instructions on how the trust's assets should be managed and distributed on behalf of the beneficiary.

But there are several crucial differences between trusts created to maintain eligibility for needs-based public assistance and those created for other reasons. With a special needs trust, the following are required to insure public assistance is preserved:

- **Sole Beneficiary.** The trust must be created for your child's sole benefit. That means nobody else is entitled to receive distributions from the trust during during your child's lifetime—not the child's spouse or children.

- **No Power to Revoke Trust.** Your child may not have the power to revoke the trust for any reason. If the trust grants the power to revoke the trust—even if that power is never exercised—it will make your child ineligible to receive public assistance. This makes sense because public assistance is predicated on a recipient's use of whatever funds are available to him or her—including assets from an available trust. If the beneficiary has the power to revoke the trust, then SSI and Medicaid will consider the trust's funds to be available resources, and they will be counted against your child.

- **No Power to Request Distributions.** If the trust grants the power to request distributions for maintenance or support, this will cause the trust's assets to be considered a countable resource for SSI and Medicaid and will cause your child to lose benefits.

- **No Direct Distributions.** It is generally advisable that the trustee not make direct distributions to your child. Instead, all distributions should be made on your child's behalf. Any money your child receives from the trust would be considered a resource. If the amount distributed exceeds the monthly resource limit on the first of the month, your child will lose eligibility until he or she spends down to below the allowable limit.

  To avoid this possibility, all distributions should be made to the third-party vendor. For example, if the beneficiary plans a vacation to New York, the trustee should pay for the tickets, hotel and other expenses directly, rather than giving the money to the beneficiary to pay.

Provided the trusts meet the legal requirements, the funds held as part of the trust will not be a countable resource for purposes of determining financial eligibility for SSI and Medicaid. There are several different types of trusts that can be created to maintain your child's eligibility for needs-based public assistance. The type created depends on your child's circumstances.

Self-Settled Trusts

A **"Self-Settled Trust (SST),"** also known as a First Party Special Needs Trust, is created either by the minor child's parent (or guardian), by the adult disabled child or via court order and funded with your child's own money. The trust's assets are only to be used to supplement your child's care. For example, they may be used to pay for: (1) medical treatment, procedures and equipment that Medicaid does not cover, and (2) other life-enriching activities that your child cannot afford because the financial requirements to qualify for assistance leave him with insufficient funds.

Despite your best efforts, there may be instances in which your child receives an outright distribution of funds that exceed SSI and Medicaid's allowable income and resource limits. Examples of this may include:

- An inheritance from grandparents or other relatives who did not put the proper safeguards on their gifts, such as failing to create a supplemental needs trust (discussed on page 51) or to leave the inheritance to a trust you created to protect benefits.

- Your child was involved in a lawsuit that resulted in a judgment or out-of-court settlement. Often these judgments arise from an accident or injury that caused the disability, but they can also arise from an unrelated lawsuit.

- Your child's disability occurred later in life and employment earnings and/or accumulated other assets put him or her over the income and resource limits, but are insufficient to cover medical costs.

Whatever the source of the funds, receipt of any money that exceeds the monthly allowable income and resource limits will cause your child to become ineligible for services. Without an SST, the only way children can regain eligibility is to spend down the assets until they fall below the applicable financial limits. The end result: Your child will have no source of money to act as a safety net in the event he or she needs medical services or equipment not covered by Medicaid, and no access to funds that will allow the participation in normal, everyday, enrichment activities that people without disabilities take for granted.

In these instances, an SST is a necessity in order to preserve your child's eligibility for SSI and Medicaid. There are three forms of SSTs; they are often referred to both by their statute number and common names.

Court-Approved Special Needs Trusts

A special needs trust can be created by court order, usually at the direction of the child's parents, grandparents, guardian or conservator. Court-approved special needs trusts are usually funded with proceeds from a settlement or judgment in a personal injury case that led to the disability. But they can be created with proceeds from non-disability related personal injury cases, for example, an auto accident that left your child with injuries, but did not result in the disability.

In addition, your child must be under the age of sixty-five and qualify as disabled when the trust is created. No funds other than your child's may ever be added to the trust.

Non-Court-Approved Special Needs Trusts

This trust is the same as the court approved special needs trust, except that the adult disabled child has the mental competency to create the trust himself, rather than having a guardian or conservator create it on his behalf. As with a court approved trust, non-court-approved special needs trusts" are only available to disabled individuals under age sixty-five.

REAL LIFE EXAMPLE

Bob is a twenty-seven-year-old man with cerebral palsy who receives SSI and Medicaid. When Bob's grandmother dies, he inherits $250,000 from her estate. This immediately puts him over the resource limit for both SSI and Medicaid, causing him to lose his benefits. Although most of Bob's medical needs are adequately covered under Medicaid, he knows that in the future he may require services, supports and equipment that Medicaid will not cover. In order regain eligibility for SSI and Medicaid, and ensure that he has funds available in the future to cover care expenses that Medicaid does not, Bob creates an SST and funds it with his inheritance.

Pooled-Income Trusts

A **"Pooled-Income Trust"** is a less commonly used trust. These trusts are managed by non-profit corporations, which typically provide services to individuals with disabilities. These trusts are available to individuals of any age.

Here's how they work: Each month, trust beneficiaries send any income in excess of the allowable monthly income and resource limits to the trust managers, along with non-medical bills that need to be paid. The trust then pays these bills, and the individual retains eligibility for public benefits. When your child dies, any funds remaining in the trust are retained by the non-profit organization and are used to pay bills for those individuals remaining in the pooled-income trust.

Medicaid Payback Provisions

While SSTs can be created to maintain your child's eligibility for needs-based public assistance, they require a provision that Medicaid will be reimbursed for any expenditures made on your child's behalf.

If the SST is created for the purpose of preserving Medicaid eligibility, it must include a payback provision. Payment will be made from trust assets, to the point that if the cost of Medicaid payments exceeds the trust's assets, there will be no money left to pass on to whomever the trust names to receive any remaining assets at your child's death. If the payback provision is not included in the trust, Medicaid will deny your child coverage.

In addition to the payback provision required in the SST, federal law requires states to seek reimbursement from the estates of Medicaid recipients age fifty-five or older for payments made to nursing homes, home- and community-based services, and hospital and prescription drug costs. States may also choose to seek repayment for additional expenditures it made on a recipient's behalf. Medicaid may also place a lien on the recipient's home during his lifetime if he is permanently institutionalized, though the lien must be removed if the recipient is discharged. You have to check the law in your state to determine how this is enforced.

The state cannot, however, seek repayment if your child is survived by a spouse, child under age twenty-one, or a blind or disabled child of any age. Also, the state may not seek recovery if it would cause an undue hardship, the definition of which varies from state to state.

The Medicaid payback provision is a serious downside to the SST. When creating a trust for a typical child, parents name one or more remainder beneficiaries—individuals who will inherit the remainder of the trust's assets after the primary beneficiary (their child) dies. In most cases, the remainder beneficiaries of a child's trust are children or siblings of a disabled child.

The SST, however, requires that Medicaid be named the remainder beneficiary. This means that when your child dies, if the amount that Medicaid paid on his behalf throughout his lifetime exceeds the value of the assets remaining in the trust, there will be nothing left to pass to the remainder beneficiaries. In the case of a court settlement, there is no way to avoid that scenario.

But when it comes to assets you choose to leave a disabled child, and then other beneficiaries, you can avoid this result by creating another type of trust known as a **"Supplemental Needs Trust (SNT)"**.

Third-Party Supplemental Needs Trust

A third-party supplemental needs trust, also known as a special needs trust, is created on the beneficiary's behalf, usually by his parents or grandparents, to hold any gifts or inheritances he may receive from his parents or other family members. Prior to the creation of the SNT, parents of a disabled child had only two options available when it came to planning for their child's future: (1) leave them an outright gift, which would make them ineligible for SSI and Medicaid if the inheritance exceeded the monthly income and resource limits, or (2) disinherit them.

As a parent, you can understand why neither of these options is attractive. In the first, children would lose their eligibility for SSI and Medicaid until they had spent it down below the allowable financial limits, at which point they would regain eligibility. But they would no longer have a means of paying for medical treatment or services and equipment that Medicaid does not cover. Children also would not have access to funds to pay for regular daily activities that could enrich their lives, such as education, cultural events or vacations.

_____

Distributions from an SNT are intended to supplement, not supplant, any needs-based public assistance your child may be receiving. This means that distributions should only be made to pay for those things that are not covered by Medicaid.

_____

Create an SNT (Not an SST) When Possible

If your child receives an outright inheritance under a Will or trust, it may be possible to petition the court for a modification of the document to allow the gift to be distributed to an SNT, rather than creating an SST on your child's behalf. The benefit of this option is that unlike an SST, SNTs do not require a Medicaid payback provision.

The option to modify the gifting instrument, however, is not always available. If you find yourself in this situation, you should contact an experienced special needs trust attorney to determine whether state law or the terms of the gifting instrument itself permit the modification.

The SNT allows parents to provide for their child's supplemental needs without endangering eligibility for SSI and Medicaid. Parents (or grandparents and other family members) state in their Wills or trusts that any gifts to the child be made to the SNT. Your child's assets may never be placed in the SNT; it can only hold gifts from third parties.

SNTs are similar to SSTs in structure. The trust must be for your child's sole benefit and he or she may not have the power to revoke or amend the trust for any reason. Either of these powers will be sufficient for SSI and Medicaid to determine that the trust's assets are available for your child's support and will result in ineligible for benefits. The trust must also prohibit the trustee from making distributions for your child's support and maintenance.

Examples of allowable distributions would include:

- Medical, dental and diagnostic procedures and treatment not covered by Medicaid or any other insurance your child may have.

- Supplemental nursing care.

- Rehabilitative services.

- Cost of housing, including paying the difference between shared and private rooms if your child is in a nursing home or other housing facility.

- Expenditures for travel, cultural and educational enrichment, such as museum outings, vacations purely for pleasure, trips to visit family, along with the cost of paying another person to accompany your child.

Trigger Feature Creates Flexibility

If your child is currently not eligible to receive SSI or Medicaid, but you anticipate that he may need these benefits in the future, a "trigger" can be built into the SNT. For example, if a child has a progressive disease that will require specialized care and support as he or she ages, the SNT can include trigger language that will allow it to operate as a non-SNT while your child is not receiving needs-based public assistance, and switch to a SNT when your child needs benefits.

In all of these cases the trustee should make payments on the beneficiary's behalf, and not to the beneficiary, to ensure that he or she is never over-resourced at the start of the month.

With a trigger feature, while your child is not eligible for SSI and Medicaid, the trustee could have the power to make distributions to your child toward health, education, support and maintenance. This standard is too broad for SSI and Medicaid's resource rule and would make your child ineligible. But if your child needs to apply for Medicaid, the trigger language would convert the trust to an SNT, and it would only allow distributions that would supplement government benefits, not supplant them.

At your child's death, any assets remaining in the trust would pass to the remainder beneficiaries, who you would select when you drafted the trust. This could be to your grandchild, to other children or grandchildren, charities, other family members—the choice is yours. If your child has the mental capacity to draft his or her own Will, you may also grant the power to state, in the Will, who should receive the remainder of the trust's assets at his or her death.

Guardianship and Conservatorship of the Adult Disabled Child

It's tough for all parents of minor children to think about appointing a guardian if they can no longer care for their child. But for parents of a special needs child, appointing a guardian is essential to avoiding a court proceeding later.

When you think of guardians, you most likely think of an aunt and uncle raising their niece after her parents died. And while this is one aspect of guardianship, guardianship for a special needs child occurs when a child with a disability becomes an adult with a disability but remains unable to care for himself or herself.

In most states children "come of age" when they turn eighteen, at which point they are considered an adult capable of making their own decisions and supporting themselves—though many parents continue to provide much of that support and guidance! Many children with disabilities grow up to become adults who, with the proper supports and pre-planning by their parents, will be self-sufficient and able to make decisions regarding their own care, support and maintenance.

Other disabled children, however, will be unable to make decisions regarding their own care, support and maintenance. They will also be unable to be self-sufficient, even with additional supports and services. These children will grow up to become adults who still rely on their parents or another adult to take care of them throughout their lifetime. In these situations, you must petition the court for guardianship.

Types of Guardianship

There are two types of guardianship: guardian of the ward (usually referred to simply as guardian) and guardian of the estate (also known as conservatorship). **"Ward"** is the legal term used to describe the person who is the subject of the guardianship.

- Guardian of the ward has decision-making authority over the ward's everyday life, including housing, medical and education. These are the same decisions you had the authority to make when your child was a minor.

- Guardian of the estate is responsible for managing the ward's financial affairs, including paying bills and applying for benefits (although this can also sometimes be handled by the guardian).

In some states guardian of the ward and guardian of the estate is a single position held by one person, unless the appointees only feel comfortable handling one aspect of the guardianship. In other states, they are separate positions and you must file a petition for each, although the proceedings will most likely be combined into one single hearing.

The basic appointment procedure is the same for each position; only the information provided to the court is slightly different. Because of the similarities—and in light of the fact that most parents petition to be their child's guardian and conservator— this chapter will use the term "guardianship" and "guardian" to include appointment as guardian of both the ward and the ward's estate.

Becoming Your Adult Child's Guardian or Conservator

In order to be appointed guardian you must prove to the court that your child's ability to receive and evaluate information or to communicate decisions is so impaired that he is unable to provide for his own health and safety.

If you are also seeking appointment as guardian of your child's estate, you must prove to the court that your child is unable to effectively manage her property and financial affairs, and either:

- The property will be wasted or dissipated if it is not properly managed, or

- The child needs the management of a conservator to ensure proper financial support.

Guardianship Proceedings

Each county has a court that handles guardianship matters. Typically these courts have information packets and a website that outlines the procedure, and it is often possible to handle these proceedings on your own. Be mindful, though, that these proceedings can sometimes be emotional, especially if your child contests the guardianship, or if another person contests your appointment. Hiring an attorney who understands the requirements and can complete and submit the paperwork can help alleviate some of that stress.

Appointment Proceedings

The first step in the appointment process is filing the petition. The petition requires that you disclose the following to the court:

- Whether you are applying for appointment as your child's guardian, conservator or both.

- Information related to your child's incapacity and why a guardian is necessary.

- Your relationship to your child.

- Whether a petition for guardianship has previously been filed in any state, or if a guardianship is currently in place.

- Name and contact information of your child's spouse, children, parent (if both are not petitioning the court for appointment) and siblings.

- Name and contact information of your child's close friends who may have relevant information.

- Names and contact information of your child's medical providers.

- Information regarding your child's finances.

Once the paperwork is filed, the court will schedule a hearing. You are allowed to have witnesses testify on your behalf; however, in uncontested cases or those cases where the need for the guardianship is clear, the petition itself, along with medical records or letters from the child's physicians testifying to his disability, may sometimes be sufficient, and no testimony will be required.

If the appointment is contested, either by the child or other family members who believe they would make a better guardian, or if the judge just wants to have a thorough hearing, the court may take testimony from you, your child's caregivers (if any), teachers, doctors or others concerning his or her mental state and the appropriateness of the guardianship, as well as your ability to play the role of guardian.

The court may also appoint a **"guardian-ad-litem (GAL)."** A GAL is an independent third-party whose role it is to make sure your child's best interests are being served. The GAL will interview all parties and listed witnesses, review medical information and make a report to the court. The GAL may also call witnesses. The court relies heavily on the GAL's report in making its decision.

In addition to the petition, you must submit a guardianship plan. This plan outlines to the court how you intend to care for your child, including:

- Where your child will live.

- Any needed medical or mental health care.

- Personal care, education or work services.

- Benefits your child currently receives, or for which you intend to apply.

- Management of your child's finances, if you have also been appointed conservator.

Duties of a Guardian

If the court grants your guardianship petition, you will have the same right to make decisions regarding your child's health and well-being as you did when he was a minor, although your child should be involved in making all decisions to the extent possible. So in many ways, your day-to-day lives will not change. As your child's guardian you will have the right to:

- **Make living arrangements.** Your child should always be placed in the least restrictive environment (LRE). As guardian you may make any arrangements necessary to keep your child in his or her home, including arranging for meal delivery, housekeeping or adult day care services.

- **Make healthcare decisions.** You may make any decisions regarding your child's healthcare, although you may not be able to consent to abortion, sterilization or organ removal unless medically necessary.

- **Make legal decisions.** This includes the right to file

lawsuits intended to protect your child's personal, civil and human rights. For example, if your child was injured in a car accident, you would have the right to sue the driver on your child's behalf. You generally cannot stop your child from voting, getting a license or getting married or divorced.

- **Handle financial affairs.** If you have the additional powers of a conservator, this may include managing and investing your ward's assets, paying his or her bills, applying for public benefits and creating self-settled trusts with any assets inherited to ensure continued eligibility for SSI and Medicaid. You may also apply for any benefits your child may be entitled to, including public assistance.

Don't Put Off Planning Your Estate

Many people put off estate planning figuring that things will sort themselves out if the worst happens. But if you have a special needs child, failing to plan is truly planning to fail your child.

An estate plan puts in writing how you want your assets to be distributed at your death. Estate plans may include a Will, a trust or a combination of both, as well as other documents that are outside the scope of this book. It may seem that setting up an estate plan for yourself has nothing to do with planning for your child's future, but with a special needs child, having a plan in place is the cornerstone for providing for your child's physical and financial future.

While estate planning is covered more fully in *Estate Planning: A Road Map for Beginners,* also from Real Life Legal™, the following raises issues relevant for parents of special needs children.

What Your Will Accomplishes

The primary role of a Will in an estate plan is to:

- Give away all of the property you own in your own name, as you choose.

- Appoint a guardian for minor children.

- Appoint an executor to oversee the administration and settlement of your estate.

- Make other provisions such as payment of debts and taxes.

When it comes to the Will of a parent with one or more special needs children, care must be taken to make sure that property is left in the best way to those children, and that a guardian will be appointed who can receive a court okay if required. As discussed previously, assets should not be left outright to special needs children – nothing they can count as available resources that eliminate public assistance – until they are spent down.

Establishing Trusts

Trusts can be created either as part of your Will (called a **"Testamentary Trust"**) or during your lifetime (called an **"Inter-vivos Trust"**). A trust can have one or more beneficiaries, but in the context of special needs planning, your child must be the sole beneficiary of his own trust, or special provisions for a special needs child must be carefully drafted so that he or she is the sole beneficiary of a sub-trust. Otherwise funds disbursed can interrupt public assistance.

If a special needs child inherits funds from parents or anyone else, and the funds are left outright to the child and not in trust, needs-based public assistance will be jeopardized.

Since many special needs children receive, or will receive, some form of needs-based public assistance, usually in the form of Medicaid, SSI or SSDI, inherited funds may cause them to exceed the strict income and resource limits that come with public assistance benefits. Exceeding these maximums can result in an immediate loss of benefits. That's why it's important to create special trusts for a special needs person to receive an inheritance.

Eligibility for these public benefits for your child can be maintained if care is taken when drafting an estate plan. A supplemental needs trust, created either as part of the Will or during the parents' lifetime, can ensure your child's continued eligibility for needs-based public assistance, while still allowing him to benefit from an inheritance.

Legacies to Special Needs Children Should Be Left in Trust for Them

Leaving an inheritance to a special needs child outright, can jeopardize any public assistance benefits the child receives. It is better to give a legacy in trust for many reasons.

When a child receives an outright gift or inheritance there is no way to reject it. Needs-based public assistance programs require that recipients apply for and receive every source of potential alternate income. So if the child's grandmother leaves her grandson an outright inheritance in her Will, Medicaid will require that he accept it (and he will be penalized for it whether he accepts it or not). That means it will reduce his benefits!

To maintain eligibility for Medicaid, the grandson will need to create a self-settled trust to hold these funds. And as discussed, SSTs require a payback provision. It is therefore very important that family members—as well as any other individual who may be inclined to leave their child a bequest in his Will—know that such funds must be placed in a supplemental needs trust and not a self-settled trust.

Nomination of Guardian and Conservator for a Child Under Age Eighteen

A guardian is the individual who physically cares for your child (the ward) when you die. A conservator is the person who is appointed to manage your child's inheritance in the event you failed to create a trust. Whether your child is under the age of eighteen or a legal adult when you die, the court must approve the nomination.

If you were appointed guardian and conservator of your adult child, through a court proceeding, you may be able to nominate a successor in your Will. The court is not bound to accept that nomination, but they will strongly favor it.

Many parents choose the same person or persons to act as both their child's guardian and conservator, but there is no requirement that you do so. Your sister may be great with your kids, but may be freer with your money than you would like her to be. (Corvettes on everybody's 16th birthday!) Your brother may be a financial whiz who shares your spending philosophy, but has no interest in raising kids.

It is perfectly acceptable to choose whomever you think would be best for each role. But again, the court cannot force someone to accept the appointment simply because you nominated them, so be sure to speak with your potential appointees ahead of time.

If the positions are separate in your state, you will want to ensure that your Will specifically states whom you want to serve in each capacity, even if it is the same person. This will avoid estranged Cousin Greg from stepping forward and petitioning the court to be appointed conservator of Junior's estate, claiming that your appointment of "your closest cousin" was not specific enough to indicate that you wanted Cousin Jennifer in charge of Junior's physical and financial affairs.

Choosing a Guardian

People often put off writing a Will because they can't agree on who will serve as guardian. How, then, do you choose a guardian? It may help to identify three or four values that are important to you, and choose the person or persons who can best instill them in your child. For example:

- If it is important that your child attend church regularly and be raised in a home that practices that faith daily, you might not want to choose your atheist brother.

- If you want your children to continue living in the family home so they do not have to attend a new school and leave their friends behind, then your sister who won't move to your home town won't be a good choice.

The same factors should be considered when selecting a conservator. Conservators must provide annual accountings to the court regarding their management of a child's money. But as long as they can prove to the court that they are acting in the child's best interest, they have complete discretion in how they disburse money for the child's care—or if they even make disbursements at all. And just because the court approves of their methods does not mean that a parent would. It is important that you choose somebody who has financial values similar to yours and your spouse's.

Concluding Thoughts

Planning and decision making when you have a special needs child is something you can't put off. Know that it's part of raising your child and do the best you can. Reach out for help when you need it.

The uncertainty of not knowing what will happen to your child after you and your spouse have passed away is a frightening thought for all parents. But if you have a special needs child, the thought is compounded because you may not know who will really step up and care when you cannot.

When your child has special needs, thinking about his or her life without you can be terrifying. But understanding all of the benefits and supports available to your child, and creating a plan to ensure he or she remains eligible for all available services, can go a long way toward making sure your child will get needed care when you can no longer provide it.

Few walk this path alone, so be sure to seek out resources to help support you and your child whenever you need it.

Additional Resources

American Bar Association, Guardianship Handbooks by State
http://www.americanbar.org/content/dam/aba/
uncategorized/2011/2011_aging_gship_st_hbks_2011.
authcheckdam.pdf

American Bar Association, Special Needs Trust Basics
http://www.americanbar.org/content/dam/aba/publishing/rpte_
ereport/te_lewis.authcheckdam.pdf

Catalyst Center, TEFRA & TEFRA Look-Alike Programs
http://hdwg.org/catalyst/cover-more-kids/tefra

Medicaid Websites

Covered Services
http://www.medicaid.gov/Medicaid-CHIP-Program-Information/
By-Topics/Benefits/Medicaid-Benefits.html

Eligibility
http://www.medicaid.gov/Medicaid-CHIP-Program-Information/
By-Topics/Eligibility/Eligibility.html

Individuals with Disabilities
http://www.medicaid.gov/Medicaid-CHIP-Program-Information/
By-Population/People-with-Disabilities/Individuals-with-
Disabilities.html

Waivers (searchable index by state and/or waiver type)
http://www.medicaid.gov/Medicaid-CHIP-Program-Information/
By-Topics/Waivers/Waivers.html

MedicaidWaiver.org (lists waivers in all 50 states)
http://medicaidwaiver.org/

Social Security Administration Websites

Benefits for Children with Disabilities
http://www.ssa.gov/pubs/EN-05-10026.pdf

Disability Evaluation Under Social Security
http://www.ssa.gov/disability/professionals/bluebook/general-info.htm

The Red Book
http://www.ssa.gov/redbook/index.html

Social Security Disability Benefits
http://www.ssa.gov/pubs/EN-05-10029.pdf

Supplemental Security Income (SSI) Benefits: http://www.ssa.gov/disabilityssi/ssi.html

Understanding Supplemental Security Income
http://www.ssa.gov/ssi/text-understanding-ssi.htm

Glossary

Activities of Daily Living (ADL): These are basic tasks of everyday life, such as eating, bathing, dressing, toileting, and transferring from sitting to standing. A person's ability when it comes to ADLs is an important factor in determining availability of public assistance benefits.

Compassionate Allowances: Medical conditions or diagnoses which meet the Social Security definition of disability.

Disability Determination Services (DDSs): The DDSs are state agencies, funded by the federal government, responsible for collecting medical evidence and making the initial disability determination.

Federal Poverty Level (FPL): Sets the standard for eligibility based on income under federal programs including Medicaid.

Guardian-ad-litem (GAL): A GAL is an independent third-party whose role is to make sure your child's best interests are being served.

Home- and Community-Based Waiver (HCBW): Medicaid waiver that allows recipients to receive respite, personal attendant, adult rehabilitation, and other services usually provided in a nursing home or long-term care facility at home or in the community.

Inter-vivos Trust: A trust that is created and funded during life, and not created under the Will of someone who has died.

Level of Care (LOC): Daily level of care required for your child to be eligible to receive TEFRA Medicaid. Must meet level of care provided in an acute care hospital, nursing facility, intermediate care facility for individuals with intellectual and developmental disabilities or an inpatient psychiatric hospital.

Medicaid: Joint Federal and State program that provides medical benefits to low-income, disabled and certain other populations.

Pooled Income Trust: Special type of trust that can be used by special needs individuals to qualify and pay for benefits for their care.

Self-Settled Trust (SST): Trust created by your child (or on your child's behalf) or by court order in order to maintain current and future eligibility for SSI, SSDI, Medicaid and other needs-based public assistance. The trust is funded solely with your child's funds.

Special Needs: Usually refers to a person who is not typical in the development of gross or fine motor skills or cognition.

Social Security Administration (SSA): Federal agency that runs the Supplemental Security Income (SSI) and Social Security Disability Income (SSDI) programs.

Social Security Disability Income (SSDI): Federal program run by the SSA. Provides benefits to disabled workers and, in some cases, their disabled children, who paid in to the system through wage contributions. Strict disability guidelines.

Supplemental Needs Trust (SNT): Trust designed to maintain your child's current and future eligibility to receive SSI, SSDI, Medicaid, and other needs-based public assistance. The trust is created and funded by a third party for your child's benefit.

Supplemental Security Income (SSI): Federal program that provides monthly benefits to individuals who are age 65 and older, blind or disabled. Strict financial and disability eligibility guidelines.

Glossary

Tax Equity Fiscal Responsibility Act (TEFRA) Waiver:
Federal law that, among other things, authorized coverage to children with disabilities whose parents do not meet traditional Medicaid financial eligibility requirements. Also known as the Katie Beckett Waiver.

Testamentary Trust: A type of trust created under your Will, which gets funded and becomes operative when you die.

Ward: Term used to describe a person who is the subject of a guardianship.

About the Author

Amy Newman, Esq.

Amy Newman is a writer and attorney living in Anchorage, Alaska. She graduated *cum laude* from The George Washington University, where she earned a dual bachelor's degree in journalism and criminal justice.

Ms. Newman attended Pepperdine University School of Law. Ms. Newman is licensed to practice law in Alaska and Illinois, and worked as an estate and trusts attorney for five years. She is the mother of two five-year-old daughters, one who has cerebral palsy.

About Real Life Legal™

Parker Press Inc., the publisher of Real Life Legal™, creates plain language consumer information on legal, tax, business and financial subjects. Taking aim at info overload and legalese, Parker Press Inc. launched Real Life Legal™ in 2014. Real Life Legal™ provides practical advice, written by lawyers, to help people understand how the law works. Our goal is to provide solid, easy-to-understand information so *you* can decide whether it makes sense to hire a lawyer. Real Life Legal™ wants you to be prepared.

Available Titles

Bankruptcy Basics: Chapter 7 and Chapter 13
Marina Ricci, Esq.

Business Owners Startup Guide
Susan G. Parker, Esq. and Lynne Williams, Esq.

Elder Law: Legal Planning for Seniors
Susan G. Parker, Esq. and Maria B. Whealan, Esq.

Employee's Guide to Discrimination and Termination
Joanne Dekker, Esq.

Estate Planning: A Road Map for Beginners
Susan G. Parker, Esq. and Maria B. Whealan, Esq.

Filing a Homeowner's Claim: Natural Disaster or Not
Dawn Snyder, Esq.

A Lawyer's Guide to Home Renovations
John A. Goodman, Esq.

Available Titles (Continued)

Planning for Pets: Trusts, Leash Laws and More
Joanne Dekker, Esq.

Planning for Your Special Needs Child
Amy Newman, Esq.

Special Needs Education: Navigating for Your Child
Lynne Williams, Esq.

U.S. Veterans: Your Rights and Benefits
Maria B. Whealan, Esq.
with Paul M. Goodson, Esq.

What to Do When Someone Dies
Susan G. Parker, Esq.

You've Been Arrested: Now What?
Maryam Jahedi, Esq.

Notes

Notes

Notes

Notes

Notes

Notes

Notes

Notes

Notes

Notes

Notes

Notes

Notes

Notes

Notes

Notes

Notes

Notes

Notes

_____

_____

_____

_____

_____

_____

_____

_____

_____

_____

_____

_____

_____

_____

_____

_____

_____

_____

_____

_____

Notes

Notes

Notes

Notes

Notes